040633

JBIOG
Suley
Greenblatt, Miriam

Suleyman the Magnificent and the
Ottoman Empire

SÜLEYMAN THE MAGNIFICENT
and the Ottoman Empire

by Miriam Greenblatt

BENCHMARK BOOKS

MARSHALL CAVENDISH
NEW YORK

ACKNOWLEDGMENT

With thanks to Side Emre, candidate for Ph.D. in the
Department of History, University of Chicago,
for her thoughtful reading of the manuscript

Benchmark Books
Marshall Cavendish
99 White Plains Road
Tarrytown, New York 10591-9001
www.marshallcavendish.com

Text copyright © 2003 by Miriam Greenblatt
Map © 2003 by Marshall Cavendish Corporation
Map by Rodica Prato

Library of Congress Cataloging-in-Publication Data
Greenblatt, Miriam.
Süleyman the Magnificent and the Ottoman Empire / by Miriam Greenblatt.
p. cm. — (Rulers and their times)
Summary: Provides an overview of the lives of Süleyman I and his subjects in the Ottoman Empire of the sixteenth
century, and includes excerpts from poems, letters, and stories of the time.
Includes bibliographical references and index.
ISBN 0-7614-1489-4
1. Sèüleyman I, Sultan of the Turks, 1494 or 5–1566—Juvenile literature. 2. Turkey—History—
Sèüleyman I, 1520–1566—Juvenile literature. [1. Sèüleyman I, Sultan of the Turks, 1494 or 5–1566.
2. Kings, queens, rulers, etc. 3. Turkey—History—Sèüleyman I, 1520–1566. 4. Turkey—Civilization—History—
16th century.] I. Title. II. Series.
DR506 .G74   2002   956.1'015'092—dc21   2002001974

Photo Research by Linda Sykes, Hilton Head, SC
Erich Lessing/Kunsthistorisches Museum, Vienna/Art Resource NY: Cover; British Library, London, UK/Bridgeman Art
Library: 5; Topkapi Palace Museum, Istanbul, Turkey/Giraudon/Art Resource NY: 6–7, 15; AKG Berlin/Superstock: 11;
Erich Lessing/Louvre, Paris, France/Art Resource NY: 13; The Art Archive/Museo Correr Venice/Dagli Orti: 17, 32–33, 39,
41, 44; Chester Beatty Library, Dublin/Bridgeman Art Library: 23, 31; Bibliotheque Nationale, Paris, France/Giraudon/Art
Resource NY: 26; Bibliotheque Nationale, Paris, France/AKG London: 35; The Granger Collection: 36; Stapleton
Collection UK/Bridgeman Art Library: 47, 52, 55; The Art Archive/Biblioteca Nazionale Marciana, Venice, Italy: 50;
University Library, Istanbul, Turkey/Bridgeman Art Library: 59; School of Oriental and African Studies Library, University
of London/Bridgeman Art Library: 61, 70; Ashmolean Museum, Oxford, UK/Bridgeman Art Library: 62; The Art
Archive/Topkapi Museum Istanbul/Dagli Orti: 64; Forschungsbibliothek, Gotha/AKG London; 66–67
Printed in Hong Kong
135642

Permission has been granted to use extended quotations from the following copyrighted works:

Nasreddin Hodja by Alpay Kabacali, illustrations by Fatih M. Durmus, copyright © 1992. Reprinted by permission of
Net Turistik Yayinlar.
Suleiman the Magnificent 1520–1566 by Roger Bigelow Merriman, Cambridge, MA: Harvard University Press.
Copyright © 1944 by the President and Fellows of Harvard College.
"The Lion's Den" from *A Treasury of Turkish Folktales for Children*, © 1988 by Barbara K. Walker. Reprinted by
permission of Linnet Books, North Haven, CT.
"Hasan, the Heroic Mouse-Child" from *A Treasury of Turkish Folktales for Children*, © 1988 by Barbara K. Walker.
Reprinted by permission of Linnet Books, North Haven, CT.
"Kayikçi Kul Mustafa" ("Ballad to Young Osman") from *History of Ottoman Poetry*.
"Mesihi" ("Quatrains on Spring") from *History of Ottoman Poetry, Vol. ii, pp. 238–241*.

Contents

The Perfect Ten

Beginning in the 700s, Turkish nomads were moving westward from the steppes of central Asia. In the 800s they reached the Arab Empire. They changed from herders to farmers and adopted the religion of Islam. Because they were such good fighters, they were recruited into the Arab army, where many of them rose to the rank of general.

In the 1000s, one group of Turks, known as the Seljuk Turks, conquered a large part of the Byzantine Empire (formerly the eastern half of the old Roman Empire). During the 1100s, the Seljuk Empire split into several smaller principalities. In the 1300s, one of these principalities began to assume control over the others. Since its ruler was named Osman or Othman, his followers become known as Ottoman Turks. In 1453 the Ottoman Turks delivered the deathblow to the Byzantine Empire by capturing its capital of Constantinople (present-day Istanbul). From there, they extended their conquests in both Europe and North Africa.

In 1520 the Ottoman ruler Süleyman I (sometimes spelled Suleiman) came to power. His subjects thought his ascension to the throne a lucky event, for Süleyman was closely associated with the perfect number ten. He had been born in the tenth century after the founding of Islam and was the tenth sultan of the Ottoman dynasty. His rise boded well, the people thought, and they were not wrong.

Süleyman the Magnificent was one of the most powerful and remarkable individuals of the 1500s.

Süleyman reigned for forty-six years, until 1566. During that time he fought thirteen major campaigns and carried the Ottoman Empire to its greatest heights of power and prestige. It is not surprising that he was called Süleyman the Magnificent.

In this book you will learn about Süleyman's campaigns on land and sea. You will read about his accomplishments in the fields of law and art. You will see how the Ottomans lived and worked. And you will read letters, poems, and stories in which they tell us about their feelings and beliefs.

PART ONE

Mounted on a horse, Süleyman leads his troops into battle. Historians have often said that the Ottoman Empire "lived for war."

"Lord of the Age"

Beginnings

Little is known about Süleyman's early years. He was born either in 1494 or 1495. His father was Selim I, known to Turks as Selim the Grim and to Europeans as Selim the Terrible. Selim I spent most of his time in the field with his army expanding the lands under Ottoman rule. As a result, Süleyman scarcely knew his father and apparently was raised by his mother, a charming, intelligent woman named Hafssa or Hafiza Khatoun.

On September 21, 1520, Selim I died, probably of cancer. According to custom, his death was kept a secret until Süleyman was able to reach the Ottoman capital of Constantinople and ascend the throne. The new sultan entered the city on September 30 to the cheers of both the army and the general population. The next day, dressed in black, he escorted his father's body to its burial place. There he ordered construction of the four buildings that were always built upon the death of a sultan: a tomb; a mosque, or Muslim house of worship; a hospital for the sick; and a hostel for travelers. He also ordered construction of a school.

Over the next few days Süleyman distributed money to his soldiers, freed prisoners, lifted a ban against products made in Persia, and executed a number of corrupt officials. The Turks and their subjects were delighted. At last, a sultan who was both firm and fair!

Europeans were likewise delighted with Süleyman. "A wise

Lord, given to much study," observed an Italian diplomat. Another Italian diplomat wrote home that "a gentle lamb had succeeded a fierce lion."

Neither the Ottomans nor the Europeans, however, realized that Süleyman had two sides to his character. He was not only just, generous, honest, and a lover of learning. He was also, as one historian has observed, "fiercely determined to be 'Lord of the Age' . . . and both willing and eager to prove his superiority by force of arms."

By Land and by Sea

It was an opportune time for Süleyman to invade Europe. The continent was in a state of political turmoil. Its two leading Christian monarchs, Charles V and Francis I, were bitter enemies.

Charles V was the Holy Roman Emperor. This made him the ruler of most of what are now Germany and Austria. He was also the king of Spain. But while his German and Spanish possessions were both large, they were separated from each other by France. What Charles V wanted was to take over French territory and create an empire that included all of western Europe.

Francis I was king of France. He felt that *he*, not Charles V, should have been chosen as the Holy Roman Emperor. And he certainly did not want to be part of an empire that Charles V headed.

To further complicate matters, Europe was in the midst of a religious revolution. For many years people had been criticizing the Catholic Church for corruption and neglect. In 1517 a German monk named Martin Luther started a movement that quickly led to the rise of Protestantism. Charles V supported the Church. Francis I, although himself a Catholic, supported the German states that had turned Protestant because doing so made Charles V less secure.

In 1521 Charles V and Francis I went to war against each other. A few months later Süleyman launched his first campaign, up the

Danube River valley into central Europe. His goal was to capture the city of Belgrade, the anchor of Hungary's southern defense line. He reached it on July 31 and captured it within a month. The Hungarians had appealed to Charles V for help in resisting the Turks. But the Holy Roman Emperor was too occupied with his own problems to do anything.

The Capture of Rhodes

With his first campaign a rousing success, Süleyman turned his attention to the island of Rhodes in the Mediterranean Sea. For two hundred years, a Christian military order known as the Knights Hospitallers of Saint John of Jerusalem had been headquartered on the island. From their fortress, the knights preyed on Muslim ships carrying Egyptian grain to Constantinople and Egyptian pilgrims to the holy city of Mecca, in what is now Saudi Arabia.

Süleyman's capture of Rhodes in 1522 was a major accomplishment. For one thing, he did not rely mostly on artillery, as he had in his attack on Belgrade. Instead he used mines placed in covered trenches and exploded with gunpowder. It was an approach that had rarely been tried in the past—but it succeeded. After a siege lasting 145 days, Rhodes surrendered, and the surviving knights left the island. (Like the Hungarians before them, the knights had appealed to Charles V for help, but to no avail.) Most of the eastern Mediterranean was now under Ottoman control.

Fighting in Central Europe

For the next three years Süleyman rested on his laurels. Then, in 1525, his army rioted. The soldiers were bored with not having any battles to fight. More importantly, battles were how they obtained loot. Süleyman put down the riot and then mobilized for a second invasion of Hungary. He was probably encouraged to do so by the fact that Francis I had been made a prisoner by Charles V. Francis sent Süleyman a secret letter, hidden in the sole of a diplomat's shoe, in which he urged the sultan to attack Charles. "For the rest of Süleyman's reign the French were either his allies or friendly onlookers."

Süleyman began his westward journey in April 1526. Torrential rains, sometimes mixed with hail, made travel difficult, and it was not until August that the Ottomans faced the Hungarian army. Once again the Hungarians had asked the Holy Roman Emperor for help, and once again aid had been refused.

Francis I was tall,
athletic, and graceful.

To make matters worse for the Hungarians, their nobles disagreed with their king about what tactics to follow. The king wanted to advance to meet the enemy. The nobles thought that would be too expensive. So they drew up their army on a marshy plain near the little town of Mohács. The nobles also refused to dig themselves in behind fortified wagons. They wanted military glory. So they charged the Ottoman line. The soldiers in the center of the line retreated, drawing the Hungarians after them. Then the two wings of the Ottoman army encircled the Hungarians, and the Turkish artillerymen pounded them with cannon fire.

It was Süleyman's greatest victory ever. Tens of thousands of Hungarians were killed, including their king. Since then, whenever a Hungarian is overtaken by a disaster, he is likely to say, "No matter, more was lost on Mohács field."

Over the next few days Süleyman's troops captured and burned the cities of Buda and Pest (today's Budapest). Then Süleyman returned to Constantinople. He resumed his campaign three years later, in 1529. This time his army made it seven hundred miles up the Danube to the walls of Vienna, the capital of Austria. However, the weather was even worse than it had been in 1526. Roads were so waterlogged that cannons could not be moved and had to be abandoned. Horses fell and broke their legs. As one historian wrote, "Nothing escaped the rain; the food was sloppy with it, weapons rusted, harness grew green with mildew, and water seeped into powder kegs and ruined them." With winter approaching and supplies running short, the sultan decided to withdraw his troops.

Süleyman came back to threaten Vienna once again, in 1532. But this time he faced a united enemy. Charles V and Francis I had made peace. So had Charles V and Martin Luther, both of whom had concluded that it was more important for Christians to stand together against the Turks than it was for Catholics and Protestants to fight against each other. As a result, the garrison at Vienna included an international force of defenders.

People often write about the siege of Vienna. There was no real siege. Süleyman did not want to launch a direct attack on the city because torrential rains had again prevented him from bringing up his heavy artillery. On the other hand, when he tried to lure Charles V into open battle, the emperor refused to fight. So instead of attacking Vienna, Süleyman withdrew for the second time.

Both sides claimed victory. And perhaps both were right. Charles V won because the Ottomans failed to capture Vienna. Süleyman won because Europeans now had, in the words of one historian, "a proper respect for Turkish arms. Here were no barbaric

It is estimated that forty thousand Turks and twenty thousand Christians died during Süleyman's siege of Vienna in 1529.

hordes from the steppes of Asia, but a highly organized modern army, such as the West, in this age, had not before encountered." For the next four-hundred-odd years, the Ottoman Empire was to be a major player in European politics.

The Campaigns of Barbarossa

Realizing that he could advance no farther into Europe, Süleyman once again turned his attention to the Mediterranean Sea. Since to date Turkish sailors had proven inferior to their counterparts in the West, Süleyman decided that a strong leader was needed to take command of the Turkish fleet. He sent for a North African pirate named Khayr ad-Din Barbarossa. Despite his name, which means "red beard," Barbarossa did not have a red beard. He took the name from his late brother Aruj (or Oruc), who *did* have a red beard.

Barbarossa arrived in Constantinople in 1533 and proceeded to turn the Ottoman navy into a first-class fighting force. The next year he carried out a series of attacks, first against the coastal towns of Italy, then against northern Africa. He succeeded in capturing the strategic port of Tunis, which commands the Mediterranean Sea between Africa and Sicily, but lost it again to Charles V.

In 1537 Barbarossa returned to the attack. He again ravaged the Italian coast and captured or plundered several dozen Greek islands at the mouth of the Adriatic Sea. The following year the Turkish fleet, with help from hurricane winds, drove the Christian fleet before it at the battle of Prevesa. The Christian fleet included ships supplied by Charles V, the city-state of Venice, and the pope.

Over the next several years Barbarossa carried the Turkish flag all the way to Gibraltar, and even beyond. Wintering at the French port of Toulon, he struck at Spain and Portugal, as well as Italy and Greece. By the time he died in 1546, the Turkish fleet was dominant throughout most of the Mediterranean.

Fighting in Asia

In addition to attacking Europeans on land and sea, Süleyman launched three campaigns eastward against Persia (present-day Iran). Although the Persians were Muslims, they followed the

The most common warship of the 1500s was the galley. Although it carried sails, rowers took over in battle. They sat three to a bench, working a thirty-five-foot-long oar. Since they were usually prisoners of war, they were chained to the galley by one leg. Living conditions aboard a galley were dreadful. The rowers could not wash themselves, and had to urinate and defecate where they sat.

Shiite branch of the religion rather than the Sunni branch that the Ottoman Turks followed. This religious difference was one reason for Süleyman's attacks. In addition, there had been frontier clashes between the two empires for some time.

Süleyman first marched against Persia in 1533. The following year he captured two important cities, Tabriz and Baghdad. His second campaign began in 1548 but proved inconclusive. His third and last campaign started in 1553 and concluded two years later. The end result was that Süleyman realized, as he had in Europe, that he could go so far but no farther. Nevertheless, the territory he conquered almost doubled the size of the Ottoman Empire and gave the Turks an outlet on the Persian Gulf. The empire now stretched from the Atlantic Ocean all the way to the Indian Ocean.

ATLANTIC

OCEAN

FRANCE

Danube River

Vienna

AUSTRIA

Buda

Pest

Sziget

Mohàcs

HUNGARY

Belgrade

SERBIA

RUMELIA

REPUBLIC OF VENICE

ADRIATIC SEA

ALBANIA

ITALIAN CITY-STATES

Toulon

SPAIN

PORTUGAL

KINGDOM
OF SICILY

Prevesa

GREECE

Tunis

MALTA

Gibraltar

MEDITERRANEAN SEA

THE WORLD OF SÜLEYMAN THE MAGNIFICENT

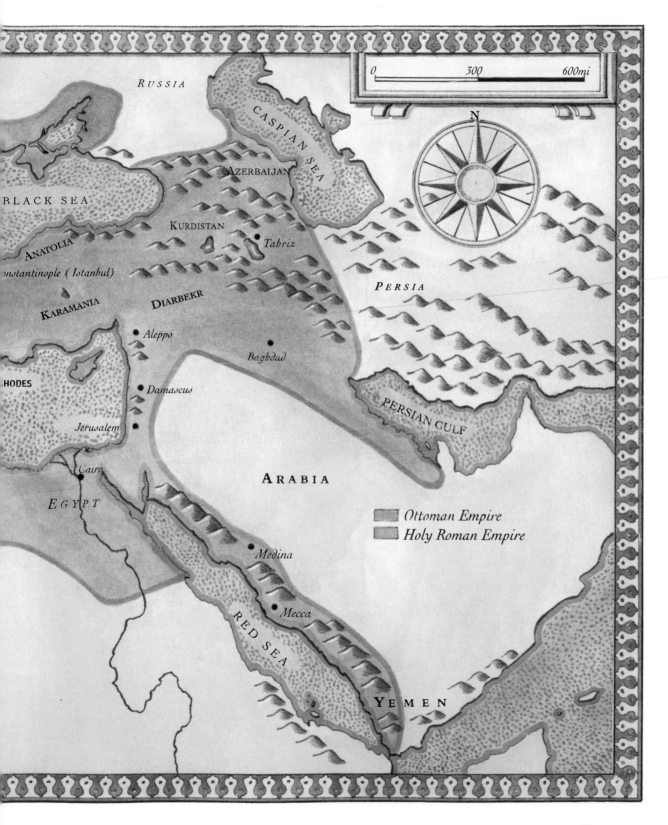

RUSSIA

CASPIAN SEA

AZERBAIJAN

BLACK SEA

KURDISTAN

Tabriz

ANATOLIA

onstantinople (*Istanbul*)

KARAMANIA

DIARBEKR

PERSIA

• *Aleppo*

• *Baghdad*

HODES

• *Damascus*

Jerusalem •

PERSIAN GULF

• *Cairo*

ARABIA

EGYPT

Ottoman Empire
Holy Roman Empire

• *Medina*

• *Mecca*

RED SEA

YEMEN

N

0   300   600mi

The Lawgiver

When Süleyman was a young boy, he learned a guiding principle called the "circle of justice." It went like this:

"To control the State requires a large army.
To support the troops requires great wealth.
To obtain this wealth the people must be prosperous.
For the people to be prosperous the laws must be just.
If any of these is neglected, the State will collapse."

Throughout his reign Süleyman paid great attention to laws. He collected all the judgments that had been issued by the nine Ottoman sultans who preceded him. He also considered existing customs. After eliminating duplications and choosing between contradictory statements, he issued a single legal code, being careful that it did not violate the basic laws of Islam.

Süleyman's code set out the duties and rights of his subjects. It laid out the relationship between Muslims and non-Muslims. It even described the clothes different people were to wear. Turkish men wore red trousers, Armenian men purple trousers, Jewish men sky-blue trousers, and Greek men black trousers.

The Ottoman Empire was very tolerant toward its religious and ethnic minorities. Non-Muslims were free to worship as they wished. No one was forced to speak the Turkish language if they did not want to. Groups such as Armenians, Jews, Arabs, and

Berbers were exempt from military service. Although required to pay a yearly tax of 10 percent, the non-Turkish communities all governed themselves. They even tried their own criminals in their own courts.

Süleyman made many changes in Ottoman law to bring it up-to-date and also to make it more humane. Fines replaced beatings as punishment for lesser crimes. Fewer people were condemned to death for severe crimes. However, forgers and false witnesses were still punished by having their right hands cut off at the wrist. No one could charge more than 11 percent interest on a loan. People were supposed to treat their animals kindly.

Süleyman's legal code was a major accomplishment. It lasted for more than three hundred years.

A Patron of the Arts

Süleyman was very interested in the arts, especially architecture. One way he promoted it was by appointing Mimar Sinan, the Ottoman Empire's greatest architect, as court architect in 1539.

Sinan built two magnificent mosque complexes in Constantinople, the Sehzade Mosque and the Süleymaniye Mosque. Each complex included—in addition to a mosque—royal tombs; several *medrese*s, or religious schools; hospitals; a soup kitchen for the poor; a bathhouse; shops; and a hostel for travelers.

Each mosque was noted for its minarets, or tall pointed towers, and, especially, for the huge dome that soared above its interior space. Oil lamps attached to a long chain dangled from the dome's center. Two rows of windows with pointed arches were set into the walls. The upper row was filled with colored glass, the lower row with clear glass. Rugs covered the floor, but there was no furniture. Blue, green, and tomato-red tiles lined the walls. The tiles were decorated with flowers, geometric designs, and writings from the Koran, the Muslim holy book.

The courtyard in front of each mosque was a busy, crowded place. There were small booths where people could buy religious objects. There were stools on which public letter writers sat while waiting for customers. Beggars crouched along the walls. Men

It took just seven years to build the Süleymaniye Mosque.
Non-Muslims were not allowed inside.

talked in the shade of the portico. And a stone-and-marble
fountain, where people washed themselves before praying, bub-
bled away.

The Royal Routine

Süleyman's daily routine when in Constantinople seldom varied. Upon rising in the morning, he was dressed by attendants who helped him don his caftan, an ankle-length tunic with sleeves that came to the wrist. Twenty gold coins were placed in one pocket of the caftan and a thousand pieces of silver in the other pocket. At the end of the day the caftan, together with the gold and silver, became the property of Süleyman's chief attendant. The sultan never wore the same caftan twice.

Unless he was attending a special feast, Süleyman usually ate his meals alone. His food, which was tasted before he ate, was brought to him on porcelain and silver dishes. A doctor always stood by his side, ready to help in the event of poisoning.

Süleyman spent much of his day consulting with officials, greeting diplomats from foreign countries, and going over petitions from his subjects. He napped in the afternoon. In his spare time he went hunting, listened to music, watched wrestling, and relaxed in his garden. He loved to read, especially books on history and religion.

Süleyman slept in a different room of his palace each night. Tall candles burned at the four corners of his red velvet couch, and four armed guards were always on duty.

Intrigue in the Harem

Like Ottoman sultans before him, Süleyman kept a harem. At first his favorite mistress was Gülbehar, or "The Rose of Spring," so-called because of her lovely complexion and graceful figure. Gülbehar was the mother of Süleyman's firstborn son, Mustafa, the heir apparent to the throne. A handsome, intelligent youth, Mustafa received an excellent education and became an able administrator. The Turkish army was devoted to him.

In the meantime, about ten years after Süleyman became sultan, a new addition to the harem attracted his attention. She was called Khurrem, or "Laughing One," because of her radiant smile and sunny disposition. Small, fair-haired, and not particularly beautiful, it was said, she had "enormous charm, great intelligence, and a will of steel." Europeans called her La Russelane because she was of Russian birth. Historians have modified that to Roxelana.

Roxelana bore Süleyman a daughter and three sons, Selim, Bayezid, and Jehangir. Jehangir had a crooked spine and was thus deemed unsuitable for the throne. Bayezid had all of his father's good qualities and few of his faults. Selim was "short, obese, ugly and incompetent," to say nothing of being a drunkard. But he was Roxelana's firstborn and, like many mothers, she refused to acknowledge his defects. She was determined that he would succeed Süleyman as head of the Ottoman Empire.

Roxelana began by having Gülbehar banished from the capital for much of the year. That removed a rival for the sultan's attentions. Then Roxelana persuaded Süleyman to marry her. It was the first time in six generations that an Ottoman sultan had taken a legal wife, and it gave Roxelana an unshakable social position. Her next step was to convince Süleyman to appoint their son-in-law, Rustem Pasha, as his grand vizier, or chief adviser. That enabled her to influence the workings of the government.

Roxelana enjoys a holiday celebration with other members of the sultan's harem.

Finally Roxelana began dropping disquieting remarks about Mustafa. He was certainly popular with the army, wasn't he? Was it possible that he would try to seize the throne before Süleyman died? After all, that was what Süleyman's father had done, and people had praised Selim I for his action. Maybe Mustafa intended to imitate his grandfather.

Süleyman had a suspicious nature to begin with, and Roxelana's remarks upset him no end. Then, in 1553, the Turks started their third campaign against Persia. Süleyman, who was almost sixty years old, did not go out with his army as usual. Instead, Rustem Pasha led the troops.

Soon after leaving Constantinople, Rustem—undoubtedly following Roxelana's instructions—sent the sultan a letter saying that he was losing control of his troops. The soldiers were complaining about Süleyman's absence. They were muttering that he was too old and feeble to continue as sultan. Why didn't he make way for his young and vigorous son? they kept asking.

That was too much for Süleyman. He left at once for Persia, where he took over command of the army. He then wrote to Mustafa and ordered him to appear in person to answer the accusation that he was attempting to usurp the throne. Mustafa's friends urged him not to obey his father's summons. Mustafa replied that if he had to lose his life, "he could not do better than give it back to the source from which it came." Besides, if he did not appear, it would be admitting to treason.

So Mustafa rode into Süleyman's camp, entered the sultan's tent—and was strangled with a bowstring by several mutes. His body was placed on a rug and exposed in front of the tent. The Turkish soldiers were so upset that they refused to eat. Süleyman then stripped his son-in-law Rustem of his titles and sent him away.

But the struggle for succession was not over. Two years later Rustem Pasha was back in office as grand vizier. The following year, 1558, Roxelana died. Overcome by grief, Süleyman paid no attention as his two remaining sons (Jehangir had died in the meantime) hurled insults at each other and gathered supporters. The next year outright war between the brothers broke out. Bayezid was defeated in several battles and fled to Persia, where he asked the shah for protection. Süleyman then offered the shah four hundred thousand pieces of gold if he would surrender Bayezid. The money, combined with the threat of another Turkish invasion, convinced the shah to give up Bayezid. Later, Bayezid, along with his five sons, was strangled. The way was now clear for Selim to be the next sultan.

The Final Years

As Süleyman grew older, he became increasingly sad and silent. He also became more superstitious. He stopped eating from porcelain and silver plates and substituted earthenware. He gave up listening to a boys' choir whose singing he had previously enjoyed. His health was poor, too. His appetite diminished. He suffered from gout and occasional fainting spells. His color was so pale that he took to covering his face with rouge to give the impression that he was still strong and vigorous.

To make matters worse, the Ottoman Empire suffered a major military setback. When the Knights of Saint John had been forced to leave Rhodes, many of them had settled on the island of Malta. From there a tiny fleet of seven red galleys waged guerrilla warfare against the Turks, occasionally seizing Turkish merchantmen. In 1565 Süleyman decided to capture the island and secure Turkish domination of the entire Mediterranean once and for all.

The struggle over Malta was bloody beyond belief. At one point the Turks beheaded their prisoners and crucified the headless bodies. In return the knights beheaded *their* prisoners and shot the heads into the Turkish lines. Casualties ran into the thousands on both sides. In addition the Turks were stricken with dysentery, enteritis, and what was probably malaria. At last the Ottomans were forced to withdraw. "The great expedition, which was to have crowned Suleiman's old age with glory," wrote one historian, "turned out to be the greatest disaster of his whole reign."

When Süleyman learned of the defeat at Malta, he was filled with rage. "Only with me do my armies triumph!" he shouted angrily. And the next year he set out at the head of his troops to fight his old enemies, Austria and Hungary. He was now more than seventy. His health was so poor that he could not even sit on a horse but had to ride in a carriage. Nevertheless he was determined to show that Turkish arms and soldiers were the finest in the world.

The end came before the Hungarian fortress of Sziget. The Turks began their siege on August 5. Following Süleyman's orders, they dug under the walls, placed a huge mine there, and fired it on September 5. The blast shattered the fortress's walls, making Ottoman victory certain. But Süleyman never received the news. He died that night in his tent. The cause is unknown; it may have been a heart attack or a stroke. In any event, his death was kept a secret for more than three weeks, as the Turkish army returned to Constantinople. Only when Selim was ready to be enthroned did the grand vizier tell the Turkish soldiers that their sultan was dead.

Süleyman had ruled for nearly half a century. His extraordinary reign may be best summed up in the words of a modern historian:

> *"Thus did Suleiman die as he had essentially lived . . . among his troops on the field of battle. . . . It was a fitting end, in the fullness of age and at the moment of victory, for a campaigning Sultan who reigned over a great military empire. Suleiman the Conqueror, the man of action, had expanded and secured it; Suleiman the Legislator, the man of order and justice and wisdom, had perfected it . . . ; Suleiman the Statesman had won for it the commanding status of a world power."*

After Süleyman died, his body was embalmed, or protected against decay, before being put into a litter and carried back to Constantinople.

PART TWO

Constantinople's markets
handled goods from many
parts of the world.

Everyday Life in the Ottoman Empire

Religious Beliefs and Practices

Almost every Turk was a Muslim. To become a Muslim, you simply had to recite, "There is no god but Allah, and Muhammad is the Prophet of Allah." Muhammad, an Arab, had founded the religion of Islam in the early 600s.

In addition to affirming one's faith, a Muslim was (and still is) required to pray five times a day; give alms, or charity, to the poor; fast from sunrise to sunset during the holy month of Ramadan; and, if possible, make a pilgrimage to the holy city of Mecca, in what is now Saudi Arabia.

Muslims said their prayers in Arabic. They recited them at daybreak, just after noon, halfway between noon and nightfall, just after sunset, and after nightfall. A Muslim could pray either at home or in a mosque. People who went to a mosque removed their shoes and washed their faces, arms, and feet before entering the building. Although both men and women could pray inside a mosque, the women had to sit apart, either in a gallery or behind a partition.

Depending on how rich they were, Muslims were expected to give between one-fifth and one-fortieth of their wealth in alms. In addition to helping the poor, alms were used to free debtors and to support holy men such as hermits and preachers.

Muslims blow trumpets to signal the end of Ramadan.

Fasting during Ramadan was especially difficult when Ramadan came in summer, when the days were long. The reason it did not fall at the same time every year was that Muslims followed a lunar rather than a solar calendar.

People usually made the pilgrimage to Mecca in large groups, both for convenience and for safety. (Women had to be accompanied by a male member of the family.) Once inside the city, they walked seven times counterclockwise around the Kaaba, a cube-shaped building covered with a black cloth on which were embroidered verses from the Koran. The pilgrims then listened to

At one time there were as many as two hundred orders of dervishes in the Ottoman Empire. Here, dervishes perform a religious dance.

a special sermon, threw seven pebbles at each of three ancient pillars, and finally bought a sheep or other animal and had it sacrificed. When male pilgrims returned home, they were entitled to wear a green turban and to be addressed as *hajji,* or "pilgrim." Female pilgrims were also called *hajji.*

Many Turks were members of various dervish orders. These orders had been formed during the 1100s and 1200s by Muslim mystics who wanted to draw closer to God. People joined the order that best suited them. Members were expected to obey their order's head, attend meetings, and live a pious life. One dervish order, the Baktashi, included women and allowed its members to drink wine, which is forbidden by Islam. The Rifai sometimes went into a trance and walked on live coals without suffering harm. The Kalendari gave up all their possessions and wandered about begging for food. The Mevlevi were intellectuals who believed music was an essential part of prayer.

People often went to pray at the grave of a miracle-working saint. Some of these graves belonged to Jewish prophets such as Noah and Joshua. Others belonged to old tribal gods. And still others belonged to holy men, including soldiers who had died fighting for Islam. Peasants usually asked the saints for such things as a house, a good harvest, or the birth of a child. Sultans usually asked for success in their military pursuits.

Governing an Empire

Except for the sultan and the grand vizier, the Ottoman Empire was not administered by Turks. Nearly all the officials who ran the government were Christian slaves who had converted to Islam. At first the Ottomans made a practice of training prisoners of war for government jobs. But after a while there developed a draft known as the *devşirme,* or "collecting."

Officers went around the Christian provinces of the empire, especially Albania, Greece, and Serbia. There they interviewed unmarried males, mostly between the ages of twelve and fifteen. Youngsters were chosen largely because they were healthy, good looking, and seemed both intelligent and moral. Only sons were rejected because they were expected to support their parents in old age. Those who had lived in cities or who knew a trade were likewise rejected. What the Ottoman Empire wanted was "unsophisticated raw material" that it could develop and train.

When the youngsters reached Constantinople, they were converted to Islam. They were then divided into groups for different kinds of service. Those chosen to serve in the government received an especially well-rounded and thorough education. First they studied languages: Turkish; Arabic, the language of the Koran; and Persian, the language of literature. They studied other subjects as

Süleyman's ministers were known as the Divan, or Council. They included both secular and religious officials. In addition to advising the sultan, the Divan acted as a law court to try high government officials. The Divan met four days a week, from Saturday through Tuesday.

well, including history, law, and religion. They learned a trade. They also learned how to ride a horse, wrestle, use weapons, and plan military strategy. By the time they had finished their education, at about the age of twenty-five, they were ready for anything the sultan required of them.

Fighting Wars

The most important part of Süleyman's army was probably the Janissary Corps. It consisted of twelve to twenty thousand infantrymen, or foot soldiers. Like the civil servants who staffed the Ottoman government, the Janissaries were slaves who had been Christians before they converted to Islam. They were chosen for the corps because they were physically strong and loved to fight. Originally they had not been allowed to marry, but Süleyman relaxed the rule.

The Janissaries were divided into several divisions that lived in barracks in peacetime and canvas tents in wartime. Each division had a symbol—an anchor, a fish, a flag, or a key—that was marked on their barracks and tents. Some soldiers even had the symbol tattooed on their arms or legs.

Life in each barracks centered on two or three copper cauldrons, or large kettles. The soldiers cooked their rations of rice in the cauldrons and sat around them in the evenings. If a cauldron was lost in battle, the officers of the barracks were dismissed from the army in disgrace.

New Janissaries received their military training from veteran Janissaries. The trainees were required to chop wood for fires, prepare the elder soldiers' meals, and look after the camels that carried food and other supplies. In exchange the veterans taught the trainees how to shoot guns, wield sabers, leap over trenches, and climb walls. When attacking an enemy, the trainees were placed ahead of the veterans. A trainee was accepted as a veteran after he had proved himself a hero on the battlefield.

When Janissaries were not fighting, they served as policemen. They were not supposed to work at a trade, but many of them did because they wanted the extra income.

Süleyman's army was well supplied. Food, fodder, and tents were transported by camels, which could carry twice as much as horses. Tailors, shoemakers, and doctors accompanied the troops. Bringing up the rear were large groups of volunteers, who hoped to loot enemy territory and, if they were especially brave or skillful, be rewarded by being allowed to join the regular army.

The head of the Janissaries was known as the Agha. In addition to commanding the Janissary Corps, he served as the chief of police in Constantinople.

The Turks were always trying to improve their military machine. They would analyze their most recent campaign and decide whether or not to adopt new tactics or add new weapons. They stockpiled food and clothing months in advance of the next campaign. And they maintained a permanent network of spies to bring them information about their enemies' strength, movements, and political situation.

City Life: Constantinople

The most important city in the Ottoman Empire was the capital, Constantinople. Not only was it the empire's political center, but because it lay partly in Europe and partly in Asia, it was also a great center of trade. One result was that its population was extremely cosmopolitan. Many of its inhabitants were not Turks or Muslims but Christians and Jews.

Life in Constantinople revolved around Süleyman's palace. It included government offices as well as private apartments, and consisted of a series of pavilions set around courtyards and surrounded by gardens. The palace also contained mosques, schools, hospitals, and kitchens. There were barracks, libraries, and fields where people played sports. There was even an area where condemned criminals were strangled or stabbed to death. A high wall separated the palace from the rest of the city.

Each day thousands of people entered the palace to attend meetings of the state councils or to petition Süleyman to hear their complaints or grant them favors. Camel caravans brought in food, weapons, and the taxes that government officials had collected. It is said that the palace kitchens employed a thousand cooks, who fed up to ten thousand people a day.

The rest of Constantinople was divided into *mahalle*s, or districts.

Each district centered on a mosque or, in non-Muslim areas, a synagogue or a church. Within each district stood houses, shops, a market, and a bathhouse. Some *mahalle*s were named after a distinguishing feature. Tophane, for example, was named after a gun foundry, while Kâğhithane was named after a paper mill. Other *mahalle*s were named for the day on which they held their weekly street market. Salipazari, for instance, meant "Tuesday Market."

Almost every *mahalle* had its own characteristics. Butchers and tanners lived in a *mahalle* that was noted for its strong odors. In contrast was the beautiful *mahalle* of Eyub, with its green cypress trees and resident storks. Roma, or Gypsies, told fortunes in Balatmahalle. Travelers from Asia usually stayed in the *mahalle* of Üsküdar, where they received forage for their horses or mules, two meals a day, and three nights' free lodging.

Most *mahalle*s also contained a large collection of street dogs. The animals were all alike: "about the size of a collie, fierce-looking, tawny, with bushy tails and pointed ears." They were usually fed by the *mahalle*'s inhabitants. Each group of dogs stayed within its own *mahalle*, which they helped keep clean by eating the slops and chewing the rubbish that filled the dirt streets. Only Constantinople's main streets were paved.

None of the city's streets had names. You found your way around by referring to some prominent structure—"half a mile west of the Galata Tower"—or to some past incident that everyone in the neighborhood knew about—"the house where Abdullah murdered his wife."

As a major center of trade, Constantinople contained numerous khans. These were a combination of hotel and wholesale offices,

Caravansaries, or hostels, dotted the roads between Constantinople and the main cities of the Ottoman Empire. They provided travelers and their animals with free accommodations and sometimes a free evening meal as well.

where traders brought their raw materials and finished goods. Sometimes the khans also served as factories, where the raw materials were turned into salable products.

There were two types of covered markets: *bedesten*s and *çarşi*s. The *bedesten*s served as banks. The *çarşi*s sold goods. Each aisle of a *çarşi* contained small shops that handled one particular kind of product: books, carpets, fabrics, saddles, and so on. In front of each shop was a wooden or stone bench where the proprietor and his customer could sit and discuss a possible purchase. *Bedesten*s closed at noon. Some *çarşi*s did, too, while others remained open until the afternoon prayer. After all the *bedesten*s and *çarşi*s had closed, the gates to the market were locked. Guards patrolled the streets at night.

Constantinople had uncovered markets as well as covered ones. The uncovered markets were known as bazaars and sold mostly food. They were usually open from sunrise to sunset, except on Friday (the Muslim sabbath), when many of them closed at noon.

Both covered and uncovered markets were patrolled by inspectors, who checked to make certain that goods were weighed and measured properly. Anyone caught trying to cheat a customer was beaten on the soles of his feet with thick wooden rods.

Housing and Furniture

The houses of city dwellers varied according to a person's rank and wealth.

Rich city dwellers lived in houses that were two or three stories high. The first floor was built of stone. The second and third floors were usually built of wood and brick. Each floor projected beyond the floor underneath. This protected the house's entrance from the sun and the rain. It also served to make the upper part of the house more spacious. Each floor contained a double row of windows. The lower row was covered with iron or bronze gratings. The upper row contained colored glass. Lead or tiles covered the sloping roof, which projected several feet over the house's walls.

Poor people lived in one-story houses. These were usually built of wood with a dirt floor. Many had a raised platform just outside the front door to keep the entrance clean. Neighboring families often competed as to which one had the higher platform.

Every house, whether its owner was rich or poor, maintained separate quarters for women. In a rich household the women often had their own building. In a household where everyone lived in a single room, the women's section was shut off by a thick felt cloth that hung from the ceiling.

Peasants lived in houses that were partly hollowed out from the slope of a hill. The earth that had been dug out of the hill was used to make the walls and roof of the front part of the house. The back part of the house was the women's quarters. The front part of the house was the main room and served as a combination kitchen, dining room, storeroom, and bedroom for the men. Next to the main room stood the cattle stable. Body heat from the animals helped warm the main room on cold winter nights.

The houses of the rich boasted carpets laid on top of rush

A wealthy official and his family enjoy a musical performance in their home.

matting. Since people took off their shoes at the door, the carpets lasted for a long time. People sat on divans that were covered with wool and velvet cushions in winter and with silk and satin cushions in summer. Additional seating was provided by piles of cushions placed on the floor. Vases and turbans were displayed on shelves. Clothes and linens were stored in cupboards.

Beds usually consisted of two or three cotton-stuffed mattresses piled one on top of the other, with a sheet spread on top. In winter people slept under a quilt. In summer they slept naked under a sheet.

The walls and ceiling of each room were carved and painted. But although the ceilings were high and the rooms cool in summer, keeping warm in winter was a problem. The only sources of heat were charcoal-burning braziers, or metal pans, that you had to keep refilling all the time.

Poor people's houses usually contained only a prayer rug, a stove, and either mattresses or rugs that were unrolled at night to make beds. There were no closets or cupboards. People tied extra clothes in bundles that they hung on the walls or piled in a corner. They did not store food but bought it as needed.

The houses of peasants were likewise sparsely furnished: some carpets and quilts, and a few leather bags for storing clothes and household goods. The carpets were known as kilims. They were made by sewing together strips of richly colored, flatly woven wool. The wool strips were also used for making saddlebags.

Food

Turks breakfasted early in the morning after reciting the first prayer of the day. Poor people ate black bread and cheese, to which they added vegetable soup in winter. The bread was heavily flavored with onions and garlic to make up for its coarse texture. Rich people's breakfasts included fruit, as well as jam and preserves on their bread.

Lunch eaten at home consisted of either leftovers or milk and yogurt. City dwellers sometimes ordered a dish of rice and mutton stew from the local cookshop. Workers unable to get home for lunch brought bread and onions with them for their midday meal.

The main meal of the day was dinner. Rich people ate a variety of rice dishes, soups, and mutton stews. Poor people were usually limited to rice. In spring and summer, however, everybody was able to add fresh fruit and vegetables to their diet.

People did not eat at a table. Instead they served themselves from a tray that was placed on a low stool. They sat on the floor, sideways to the tray, with the right leg raised at the knee and the left leg stretched out flat.

Serving ware consisted of spoons and either metal or wooden plates or large pieces of flat bread. People used the spoons only for soup. They ate the other food with three fingers, so it was usually served cut up into small pieces. You ate rice by taking a handful from the dish and pressing it into a ball before putting it into

Foreign envoys to Süley-man's court are entertained at an elaborate banquet.

your mouth. The meal finished with a drink of either water or fruit juice.

Turks loved sweets but, except at banquets and wedding parties, rarely ate them with meals. Between meals, however, people stuffed themselves with pastries sweetened with honey or *pekmez* (a thick molasses made from grape sugar).

Clothing and Jewelry

A typical Turkish man wore a shirt and trousers, with a wide sash tied around the waist. He tucked his tobacco into the sash but kept his money in the breast of the shirt. A rich man covered his shirt and trousers with a caftan. Students and religious scholars dressed in long black gowns.

Indoors, men wore soft-soled leather slippers over leather socks that were attached to their trousers. To go out, they put heavy yellow leather shoes on over the slippers. If they were going horseback riding, they put on loose black boots.

On their heads, poor men wore caps or cloths. Members of the clergy wore gold-embroidered skullcaps wound round with white muslin, forming somewhat flat turbans. Rich men wore high turbans made by winding white muslin around tall felt caps.

Men usually shaved their heads. Religious leaders, as well as many teachers and members of the ruling elite, were bearded.

A rich woman wore full trousers and an embroidered gauze smock with a high neck and elbow-length sleeves. Over this she put a long-sleeved waistcoat and a close-fitting caftan tied with a sash. In winter she added a brocade robe lined with fur, and a tasseled cap. Like men, well-to-do women wore leather slippers over leather socks indoors. Poor women wore just trousers and a

A well-dressed upper-class woman plays the zither.

smock. They usually went barefoot in the house but put on slippers
and overshoes when they went outdoors. Both rich and poor
women wore felt caps with kerchiefs draped on top.

Men seldom wore jewelry except for rings. Women, on the
other hand, wore as much jewelry as their husbands could afford,
including strings of pearls or gold coins that dangled from their
head scarfs.

The Ceremonies
of Life

Although Turkish families preferred boys to girls, the most important thing was that a baby be healthy. Accordingly, parents went to great lengths to protect their infants against the evil eye, a presumed power that they believed brought illness and bad luck.

About two months before a baby was due to be born, its parents collected swaddling bands, a cotton smock, a blue shawl, a bonnet, and an amulet, or charm, made of blue beads. After sprinkling the items with sesame seeds, the parents tied them in a bundle, which they hung on a wall in the direction of Mecca. Above the bundle they hung a bag containing a Koran.

A few days before the time of birth, the midwife brought her walnut birthing chair into the house. The mother gave birth sitting on the chair, while the midwife and neighboring women chanted *"Allahu akbar"*—"God is great."

As soon as the baby was born, it received a first name. After it had been washed and dressed, the amulet was pinned to its shoulder. Other defenses against the evil eye included a Koran hung over the mother's bed; onions, garlic, and blue beads, which were placed under the bed; and a broom, which stood next to the bed. Also next to the bed stood a bottle of sherbet tied with red gauze. If the gauze was tied around the bottle's neck, that meant the baby was a boy. If the gauze was tied over the bottle's top, that meant the baby was a girl.

Mothers usually stayed in bed, receiving friends who brought gifts, for several days. During this time the head of the family gave the baby a second name. This was either the name of a legendary hero or a historical personage. Turks did not have family names. However, they were identified as coming from a certain region or following a particular trade. Thus you might be known as Hassan Ali from Cappadocia or Mustafa Baba the Shoemaker.

On the seventh day after the birth many families threw a party. The maternal grandmother presented the infant with a cradle, and people sang and chanted from the Koran. On the fortieth day after the birth the new mother took her infant to the local bathhouse, accompanied by the midwife and friends. After the baby had been shown to everyone, the midwife performed the "forty" ceremony. She washed the baby with a soft soapy cloth and rubbed it with a broken duck's egg. This was supposed to keep the child safe whenever it went swimming.

Marriages were arranged between families. With few exceptions, the bride and groom did not even see each other until after the wedding.

When a boy reached marriageable age (determined by his father), his mother chose a wife for him. She asked relatives, friends, and sometimes a matchmaker about suitable brides. Then she visited their houses and examined the girls. (A girl was considered marriageable at the age of twelve.) After she made her choice, the girl's father checked into the boy's financial position and his future prospects. The most important thing was whether the two families were compatible. A father often wanted a son-in-law who worked at the same occupation as himself. The marriage contract listed such items as the size of the bride's dowry and how much money the groom's family would contribute to the cost of the wedding.

Weddings were usually held on a Friday. Unless the family was very poor, festivities started on the Monday before, when the groom received his wedding outfit from the bride's family. On Tuesday the bride visited the local bathhouse, walking under a silk canopy accompanied by musicians and friends. After she was bathed and perfumed, everyone went back to her house for a party.

On Wednesday there were two parties, one at the bride's house, the other at the groom's house. The party at the bride's house was called Henna Night because henna, an orange paste, was smeared on the bride's hands and feet for good luck. The party at the groom's house was a typical bachelor party, complete with music and dancing girls.

Thursday was a solemn day for the bride, since it marked the real end of her childhood. After dressing herself in clothes she had received from the groom, she stuck sparkling sequins on her forehead, cheeks, and chin. Her father tied a shawl around her waist and held out his sword for her to jump over,

Before her wedding day, a bride visited the local bathhouse.

saying, "Bring forth offspring who will use this sword well, like your ancestors."

On Friday the bride went to the bridal chamber in the groom's house. The groom went to the mosque, where the marriage ceremony took place without the bride being present. The groom then returned home and entered the bridal chamber. The bride removed her veil, and the couple saw each other for the first time. The groom gave his new wife a "face-see" gift and then rejoined the men for a wedding feast. The bride had her own wedding feast in a separate room. Both meals included the typical wedding dish of rice that had been colored yellow with saffron.

When a Turk died, the body was washed. Cotton wool was placed in the ears, nose, and mouth; ankles were tied together and hands laid on the breast; and the body was wrapped in a shroud. The funeral was held either the same day a person died or the next morning. On the way to the burial ground the mourners carrying the body stopped in a mosque, where prayers were said.

At the burial place the body was put into a hole with its head turned in the direction of Mecca, and the hole was covered with a large flat stone. Later two upright stones were placed at the grave's head and foot. Engraved on these stones were the deceased's name, titles, and parentage. A man's tombstone also carried a carving of the turban he had worn in life. A woman's tombstone carried either a knob or a carved decoration of flowers or leaves. It was customary to plant cypress trees near graves because they gave off a fragrant aroma. The tombstones themselves, however, were not maintained. As a result, since ground sinks over time, many tombstones soon began to lean to one side.

Medical Matters

An Ottoman Empire hospital was usually situated near a *medrese* that included a medical school. The students at the medical school worked with the doctors at the hospital. Some hospitals had a special section for mental patients that contained soothing fountains and a place for musicians who played soft music.

Many people, however, preferred to consult holy men and wisewomen rather than doctors. The holy men and wisewomen specialized in ways to protect patients from the evil eye. These included blowing on knots and burning hair. The holy men and the wisewomen also used certain remedies that were quite effective. For example, they administered rhubarb as a laxative and aniseed as an aid to digestion. Eating a mixture of herbs served to restore a person's appetite, while smoking certain herbs helped to relieve chest congestion.

The worst diseases that struck the Ottoman Empire were malaria and plague. However, what particularly upset women was not being able to have babies. As one historian explains, "Barrenness . . . was considered the greatest disgrace and misfortune that a woman could suffer."

Getting an Education

Education started at the age of five. Children learned the rituals of Islam and listened to legendary stories about the Turkish past.

When a boy turned seven, he either studied at home with a private tutor or went to a school attached to the local mosque. First he learned the alphabet. Then he memorized the Koran. The school consisted of a single room, with the teacher's desk at one end. The teacher sat cross-legged on a cushioned seat. Pupils sat cross-legged on the floor. Discipline was strict. If a boy misbehaved, he had to stand on one leg with his hands in the air. If the offense was serious, the teacher beat him with a rod.

Most boys went to work at the age of twelve. Some, however, continued their education, studying such subjects as arithmetic, ethics, and Arabic and Persian grammar. A few boys went on to a *medrese,* where they received free room and board and also a monthly allowance. The *medrese*'s curriculum dealt mostly with religion, although medicine was also taught in some places. However, the teachers—all of whom were clerics—were so conservative that they considered the printed word irreligious. To them, the only way to learn anything was to recite it by heart.

Girls did not attend school. Their mothers taught them sewing, embroidery, and the necessary prayers and legends.

In 1557 Süleyman founded an astronomical observatory in Constantinople. Among the instruments used was the astrolabe, which a scholar (*upper right*) holds up for view here. The astrolabe served to determine such things as the movement of the planets and the size of the earth and was used in navigation. It was also used to cast people's horoscopes.

Earning a Living

Work was highly respected in the Ottoman Empire. Even sultans had to learn a craft. Süleyman, for example, was a trained gold-smith. So was his father. Other sultans were gardeners, poets, and arrow makers.

Each craft was controlled by a guild. The guilds determined how many men could practice the craft and where they could perform their work. This protected workers from too much compe-tition. The guilds also set quality standards and maximum prices. This protected consumers against shoddy or overly expensive merchandise. The main drawback to the guild system was its conservative nature. Because guilds did not like change, it was extremely difficult to improve a product.

Guilds had other responsibilities in addition to regulating work. They made loans to guild members. They helped guild members who fell ill and paid for their funerals when they died. They distributed food to the poor. And they sponsored readings of the Koran at the local mosque.

The members of a guild included masters, journeymen who were studying to become masters, and ordinary apprentices. A journeyman studied with a master for several years. When he was ready, he showed examples of his work to the guild council. If the council approved them, he was taken into the guild at a special ceremony held at his father's house. The objects he had made were then auctioned off at prices high enough to enable him to set up his own shop.

Some guilds consisted of workers who were not craftsmen. For example, there were guilds of public scribes, owners of book-stores, doctors, poets, clerics, water carriers, and entertainers. There were even guilds of beggars and of thieves.

Each guild had a patron saint, and each shopkeeper kept a verse about his saint hanging in his booth. For instance, Noah was the patron of merchants and sailors, Ishmael of hunters, Anas ibn Malik of police officers, and Jesus of travelers.

A turban maker often used silk for his wares.

An Artistic People

One of the great Turkish arts was miniature painting. It was used mostly to illustrate books. The most common books were, of course, Korans and their commentaries. But there were also books about history, collections of poems, and travel accounts. Each book consisted of several folded bundles of ten pages each, placed inside a leather case. Writers used reed pens and kept their writing straight by pressing the paper pages against a card that had even rows of string stretched across it.

The Turks were also known for weaving beautiful carpets and other textiles. The carpets were made of silk or wool. Patterns included flowers, vines, and leaves. A deliberate mistake—such as a few knots of white in a red section—was made in each carpet to avoid the envy of the evil eye. Fabrics were usually woven of silk, sometimes mixed with flax. The Turks used wide looms for weaving fabrics for divan covers. Narrow looms produced fabrics for clothing and pillows.

The Turks were noted for their beautiful ceramic tiles. The most popular colors were blue and white, although red, purple, yellow, and green were also used.

Having Fun

The Turks loved music. Süleyman's court included singers and instrumentalists. Musicians played at weddings and processions. Picnic and boating parties always featured group singing as well as solo performances.

The principal musical instruments were the *kemençe*, a kind of violin; the *kanun*, a sort of dulcimer, usually made of walnut; the seven-stringed lute; and the *ney*, or flute, which was usually made of reed or cane. Drums ranged in size from the huge kettledrum, which was made of copper, to the *darbuka*, an earthenware pot shaped like an hourglass with sheepskin or goatskin stretched across one or both of its ends. The Turks also played several clicking instruments, including castanets and wooden spoons.

Many government officials had *mehters*, or army bands, assigned to them. The bands' instruments included cymbals, drums, fifes, and tambourines. Süleyman's *mehter* numbered ninety musicians, who woke the inhabitants of the palace each morning for the dawn prayer. They also performed following the daily afternoon prayer, as well as after the noon prayer on Fridays and holy days. The Janissaries always paraded to the beat of a special *mehter*. The beat went: "one, two, three—pause; that is, left, right, left, then a rest for the fourth beat with the back foot held high in position slightly raised, then a right, left, right, rest, and so on."

In addition to music the Turks loved dancing. This was especially

*Mehter*s often performed on special occasions, such as this one in honor of the sultan. The Janissary *mehter* always played at various places in Constantinople on the day pilgrims left for Mecca.

true in rural areas. People danced at family celebrations, the changes of the seasons, and agricultural activities such as planting and harvesting.

Some dances were performed in a line; others in a semicircle. Men and women usually danced separately. If they danced together, they never touched each other. Instead, they shared a handkerchief or a stick. When dancing, people always wore their best clothes and covered their heads.

Some dances imitated the actions of animals, such as an eagle pouncing on its prey. Other dances imitated natural features, such as flowing water. Still other dances dealt with battles. Then the dancers kept moving faster and faster, until they ended by leaping over a fire. Dervishes performed whirling dances in which they formed two circles, one inside the other, and spun around and around. They centered themselves by using a nail held between two toes as a pivot around which they whirled.

Turks greatly enjoyed visiting the public baths found in Constantinople and other cities. Sometimes there were separate baths for men and women, but usually women could use the baths only on certain days. Admission was free, but it was customary to leave a small tip for the attendant. People spent at least an hour in the baths. In addition to bathing with both hot and cold water, they gossiped, ate, and drank coffee with their friends.

Although the Koran disapproves of drinking wine, the Ottoman Empire was filled with public bars. However, people never drank wine at home.

Young men liked to take long walks in the countryside and also practiced such sports as archery and the *jerid*, "a game in which the participants hurled light javelins at one another from the backs of galloping horses." Gardening was popular, for the Turks were extremely fond of flowers. Soldiers on the march always made a detour to avoid trampling on roses.

PART THREE

A rare miniature painting of an elephant. The Ottoman Turks were very fond of animals, especially cats, dogs, and storks.

The Ottoman Turks in Their Own Words

Süleyman preferred handling diplomatic matters by word of mouth rather than by written statements. Whenever he had to write a letter, he used a lot of flowery phrases without being specific about anything important. A good example of his style is the following letter, which he wrote to King Francis I of France, then a captive in Spain:

By the grace of the Most High, whose power be forever exalted [glorified]! By the sacred miracles of Mohammed (may the blessing of God be upon him!), who is the sun of the skies of prophecy, star of the constellation of the Apostles, chief of the company of prophets, guide of the hosts of the elect; by the cooperation of the holy souls of his four friends, Abu Bekr, Omar, Othman, and Ali (may the blessing of God on High rest on them all!), and of all God's chosen people, I who am the Sultan of Sultans, the sovereign of sovereigns, the dispenser of crowns to the monarchs on the face of the earth, the shadow of God on earth, the Sultan and sovereign lord of the White Sea and the Black Sea, of Rumelia and of Anatolia, of Karamania, of the land of Rum, of Zulkadria, of Diarbekir, of Kurdistan, of Azerbaijan, of Persia, of Damascus, of Aleppo, of Cairo, of Mecca, of Medina, of Jerusalem, of all Arabia, of Yemen, and of many other lands which my noble forefathers and my glorious ancestors (may God light up their tombs!) conquered by the force of their arms, and which my August Majesty has made subject to my flaming sword and my victorious blade, I, Sultan Suleiman Khan, son of Sultan Selim Khan, son of Sultan Bayezid Khan: To thee who art Francis, king of the land of France.

You have sent to my Porte [court], refuge of sovereigns, a letter by your faithful agent Frangipani, and you have furthermore intrusted to him sundry verbal communications: you have informed me that the enemy has overrun your country and that you are at present in prison and a captive, and you have asked aid . . . for your deliverance. . . .

There is nothing wonderful in emperors being defeated and made prisoners. Take courage then, and be not dismayed. Our glorious predecessors and our illustrious ancestors (may God light up their tombs!) have never ceased to make war to repel the foe and conquer his lands. We ourselves have followed in their footsteps, and we have at all times conquered provinces and citadels of great strength and difficult of approach. Night and day our horse is saddled and our sabre is girt [prepared for action].

May God on High promote righteousness! May whatsoever He will be accomplished! For the rest, question your ambassador and be informed. Know it to be thus. Written in the first decade of the moon of Rebiul-akir, in the year 932 [February 1526] from the residence of the capital of the Empire, Constantinople, the well supplied and the well guarded.

Among the topics popular with Turkish poets was nature. The following poem was written by Mesihi, a government worker in Constantinople. His birthdate is unknown; he died in 1512:

Hear the nightingale declaiming! now we're in the days of spring.
Not a garden but exhibits frenzy in its phase of spring,
Almond blossoms scattered thereon in the spendthrift ways of spring.
Taste their pleasures while you're able; pass they must these days of spring.

Field and garden once again a fancy dress of blooms contrive,
On the lawns the flowers set pavilions where delight shall thrive.
Can we know when next the spring comes who'll be dead and who alive?
Taste their pleasures while you're able; pass they must these days of spring.

Another popular topic with Turkish poets was war. The following "Ballad to Young Osman" was written by Kayikçi Kul Mustafa, a member of the Janissary Corps. He lived during

The official trumpeter of the Janissary band begins to sound a note.

the 1600s and took part in the many campaigns about which
he wrote:

> *When first we marched on Baghdad town,*
> *Young Osman leapt across the moat,*
> *The flag the fallen bearer dropped*
> *He hoisted on the castle wall.*
>
> *Saddle both my dappled greys,*
> *That I may ride against the foe!*
> *Before the morning prayers were said,*
> *Young Osman swept through the city gates.*
>
> *Said Sultan Murad, send him to me,*
> *This hero of whose deed I've heard,*
> *Three-horsetail rank shall I confer*
> *On Young Osman with the bloodstained sword.*
>
> *Kul Mustafa was on patrol*
> *When cannon balls rained on our side,*
> *When cursed Baghdad claimed its toll,*
> *Young Osman led the brave who died.*

One of the few professions open to Turkish women was that of
storyteller. Storytellers would come to a house; stay for about a
week, telling the women and children stories every night; and
then move on to another house.

Many of the stories were fairy tales about kings and princesses.
English fairy tales usually start, "Once upon a time." Turkish fairy
tales generally open like this: "Once there was and once there was

not, in the time before, when the camel was a street crier and I was rocking my father's cradle." Instead of "They lived happily ever after," Turkish fairy tales usually end with the words, "They had the wish of their hearts, and may we climb the ladder of ours."

Some Turkish stories were animal folktales that gave advice on how to behave. An example is the following folktale, called "The Lion's Den":

Once the lion, king of all the animals, assembled his subjects and asked them this question: "How does my den smell?"

After a timid silence, a dog spoke up. "Your Majesty," said the honest but unwise dog, "it smells rather unpleasant. In fact—forgive me, but it stinks!"

"How dare you!" roared the lion, and, springing upon the dog, he tore him to bits.

Then the lion repeated the question. This time an eager monkey ventured: "Sir, your honorable den smells like the very roses that bloom in palace gardens!"

"Oh?" said the lion. "Well, for this false flattery, you deserve the same treatment as the dog," and he destroyed the monkey, also.

The question was this time directed at the sly fox. "Your Majesty," replied the fox, "for some time now, I've had a bad cold and I really can't tell . . ." and saved his precious life, of course.

Another favorite subject of Turkish folktales was the rejected but ultimately successful youngest child. A variation of this theme is found in "Hasan, the Heroic Mouse-Child":

Once there was and once there wasn't a man who had no child. Oh, he and his wife wanted a child, but none came. At last his wife prayed, "O Allah, send us a child, even if it be no bigger nor better than a mouse."

That day, the ears of Allah were open, and in good time the woman gave birth to a child. Nothing but a mouse he was, small and gray, with wise eyes and twitching whiskers. The neighbors were surprised, but the man and his wife were glad to have any child at all, and they named him Hasan.

As the child grew, he helped more and more around the house, and his parents rejoiced in their lively son.

One morning as the good woman was preparing a hot lunch for her husband, Hasan stood up tall on a stool. "See how big I am, my mother," he said. "Let me take the lunch to my father in the field."

"You are big, my dear," answered his mother, "but you are not quite big enough to manage our donkey while he carries the lunch to the field."

"Listen, my mother," said Hasan. "I can say 'Deh' and 'Chush' as well as the rest, and the donkey knows me well. If I am high on his back, the donkey will go and stop for me. I can ride in the saddlebag. You'll see!"

So Hasan's mother put the lunch in a tin box and tucked it into one pocket of the saddlebag, and she helped Hasan into the other pocket.

"Deh!" called the mouse-child, and off the donkey started for the field.

Hasan's father was surprised to see the donkey coming all by himself to the field. "Aman!" he exclaimed. But just as he was about to take to his heels with fear, "Chush!" shouted Hasan. And there stood Hasan, peeking over the edge of the saddlebag, with his bright eyes watching his father's surprise.

His father laughed and helped him down, and the two ate a good hot lunch together.

When it was time for his father to work again, the mouse-child scrambled up into the saddlebag. "Deh!" he shouted, and off went the donkey toward home.

On their way home, they came to the village fountain. "Chush!" shouted Hasan, and the donkey stopped. "You must be thirsty, my donkey," said the mouse-child. "Have a good drink while I climb to the top of that poplar tree. If I'm up high, I can see how the whole village looks!"

Leg over leg, Hasan climbed to the top of the tree. "Ah! Indeed I can see the whole village!" he said to himself.

Suddenly Hasan saw three men behind a bush near the fountain. They were counting: "One, two, three, one, two, three, one, two, three." And they were counting gold coins!

"Hmmnn!" said Hasan. "If they are hiding behind that bush, those may be stolen coins. I'll soon find out."

And boldly Hasan began to whistle the tune the village watchman whistled as he came down the street.

Startled, the three men looked this way and that, but they could not see the watchman. Frightened, they shoved the sack of gold coins into a hole under the bush. Then they ran out of the village as fast as they could go.

As soon as they had gone, Hasan scrambled down the poplar tree. "I can't lift that sack, but I can lift those coins one by one," he said.

And, one by one, Hasan carried the coins to the saddlebag of the donkey and dropped them, Clink! Clink! Clink! into the pocket.

As soon as all of the coins were safe in the saddlebag, Hasan pushed the empty sack down deep, deep, deep in that hole under the bush.

Then, climbing into the other pocket of the saddlebag, Hasan shouted "Deh!" and off the donkey trotted toward home.

"Chush!" called Hasan as the donkey came to Hasan's house, and the donkey stopped. Hasan's mother came to the door.

"Hasan!" she said. "I was afraid you were lost!"

Hasan laughed. "No, Mother. I was not lost. But I found something very useful. Come and see!" And he scrambled over to the other pocket of the saddlebag.

When the mother saw the gold coins, she could scarcely believe her eyes. And she was even more surprised when Hasan told her how he had frightened the robbers. "My mother," said Hasan, "even a mouse-child can make himself tall enough to help his parents."

It wasn't long before the man and his wife and the mouse-child were living in a fine new house. And, just for Hasan the hero, the house had a little balcony on top, so that Hasan could watch all the people come and go.

You see, you never can tell what will happen when you ask for a child no bigger than a mouse!

Nasreddin Hodja may or may not have been born either in the 1200s or the 1300s. Most sources say that he was a real person who served as a religious leader, a judge, and a university professor. In any event, he is the most popular story character in Turkish literature. Thousands of stories about him have been written over the centuries. Some are humorous, others are serious. But all of them tell you something about Turkish society:

WE ARE EVEN

One day, Hodja went to a Turkish bath but nobody paid him much attention. They gave him an old bath robe and a towel. Hodja said nothing and on his way out he left a big tip. A week later, when he went back to the same bath, he was very well received. Everybody tried to help him and offered him extra services. On his way out, he left a very small tip.

"But, Hodja," they said, "is it fair to leave such a small tip for all the attention and extra services you received?"

Hodja answered:

"Today's tip is for last week's services and last week's tip was for today's services. Now we are even."

Glossary

affirming: Declaring something to be true.

artillery: Large mounted guns that are fired by a crew rather than an individual.

barracks: The permanent buildings in which the Janissaries lived when they were in Constantinople.

cosmopolitan: Containing people from different parts of the world.

dowry: The money or property that a bride brings to a marriage.

dulcimer: A stringed instrument, played by plucking or strumming.

dynasty: A series of rulers from the same family.

harem: The wives and mistresses of a Muslim man.

javelin: A five-foot-long wooden spear with an iron point; when it struck a shield, the point would bend at the neck, thus preventing the enemy from pulling out the spear and throwing it back at the attacker.

Koran: The holy book of the Muslims.

medrese: A Muslim religious school.

moat: The ditch around a castle.

mute: A person who is unable to speak.

mystic: Someone who seeks direct personal experience of the divine.

pavilion: A light, roofed structure.

saber: A single-edged, curving sword used for slashing.

scribe: A writer who copied out books, letters, or documents; he also wrote down things that were dictated to him.

shah: The king of Persia.

steppes: Treeless plains covered by tall grasses.

sultan: The king of certain Asian countries.

swaddling bands: A baby's wrappings.

tunic: A loose-fitting garment, either sleeved or sleeveless.

For Further Reading

Addison, John. *Suleyman and the Ottoman Empire.* San Diego: Greenhaven Press, 1980.

Kabacali, Alpay. *Nasreddin Hodja.* Istanbul: Net Turistik Yayinlar, 1992.

Walker, Barbara K. *A Treasury of Turkish Folktales for Children.* Hamden, CT: Shoe String Press, 1988.

ON-LINE INFORMATION*

http://www.cs.umd.edu/users/kandogan/FTA/Art/Miniature/miniature.html
Miniature Collection: "The Age of Sultan Suleyman, the Magnificent" Exhibition.

http://www.osmanli700.gen.tr/english/sultans/10index.html
Ottoman Web Site: Kanuni Sultan Süleyman.

http://www.allaboutturkey.com/suleyman.htm
Süleyman, The Magnificent.

*Websites change from time to time. If you cannot find what you are looking for, use a search engine and type in a keyword. Or check with the media specialist at your local library.

Bibliography

Addison, John. *Suleyman and the Ottoman Empire.* San Diego: Greenhaven Press, 1980.

Bridge, Antony. *Suleiman the Magnificent.* New York: Franklin Watts, 1983.

Goodwin, Jason. *Lords of the Horizons.* New York: Henry Holt, 1999.

Kabacali, Alpay. *Nasreddin Hodja.* Istanbul: Net Turistik Yayinlar, 1992.

Kinross, Lord. *The Ottoman Centuries.* New York: William Morrow, 1977.

Lamb, Harold. *Suleiman the Magnificent.* Garden City, N.Y.: Doubleday, 1951.

Lewis, Raphaela. *Everyday Life in Ottoman Turkey.* New York: G . P. Putnam's Sons, 1971.

Menemencioğlu, Nermin, ed. *The Penguin Book of Turkish Verse*. New York: Penguin Books, 1978.

Merriman, Roger B. *Suleiman the Magnificent*. New York: Cooper Square Publishers, 1966.

Walker, Barbara K. *A Treasury of Turkish Folktales for Children*. Hamden, CT: Shoe String Press, 1988.

Notes

Part One: "Lord of the Age"

Page 8 "A wise Lord": Lamb, *Suleiman the Magnificent*, p. 17.
Page 9 "a gentle lamb": Goodwin, *Lords of the Horizons*, p. 81.
Page 9 "fiercely determined": Bridge, *Suleiman the Magnificent*, p. 39.
Page 12 "For the rest of Süleyman's reign": Addison, *Süleyman and the Ottoman Empire*, p. 11.
Page 13 "No matter": Kinross, *The Ottoman Centuries*, p. 187.
Page 14 "Nothing escaped the rain": Bridge, *Suleiman the Magnificent*, p. 113.
Page 14 "a proper respect": Kinross, *The Ottoman Centuries*, p. 196.
Page 20 "To control the State": Bridge, *Suleiman the Magnificent*, pp. 29–30.
Page 25 "enormous charm": Bridge, *Suleiman the Magnificent*, p. 112.
Page 25 "short, obese": Bridge, *Suleiman the Magnificent*, p. 163.
Page 27 "he could not do better": Kinross, *The Ottoman Centuries*, p. 239.
Page 29 "The great expedition": Bridge, *Suleiman the Magnificent*, p. 188.
Page 30 "Only with me": Kinross, *The Ottoman Centuries*, p. 251.
Page 30 "Thus did Suleiman": Kinross, *The Ottoman Centuries*, p. 255.

Part Two: Everyday Life in the Ottoman Empire

Page 38 "unsophisticated raw material": Lewis, *Everyday Life in Ottoman Turkey*, p. 25.
Page 43 "about the size of a collie": Goodwin, *Lords of the Horizons*, p. 324.
Page 56 "Bring forth offspring": Lewis, *Everyday Life in Ottoman Turkey*, p. 103.
Page 57 "Barrenness": Lewis, *Everyday Life in Ottoman Turkey*, p. 107.
Page 63 "one, two, three—pause": Lewis, *Everyday Life in Ottoman Turkey*, p. 160.
Page 65 "a game": Merriman, *Suleiman the Magnificent*, p. 201.

Part Three: The Ottoman Turks in Their Own Words

Page 68 "By the grace of the Most High": Merriman, *Suleiman the Magnificent*, pp. 129–131.
Page 70 "Hear the nightingale declaiming!": Menemencioğlu, *The Penguin Book of Turkish Verse*, p. 74.
Page 71 "When first we marched": Menemencioğlu, *The Penguin Book of Turkish Verse*, p. 147.
Page 72 "Once the lion": Walker, *A Treasury of Turkish Folktales for Children*, p. 16.
Page 73 "Once there was and once there wasn't": Walker, *A Treasury of Turkish Folktales for Children*, pp. 8–10.
Page 76 "One day, Hodja went to a Turkish bath": Kabacali, *Nasreddin Hodja*, p. 16.

Index

Page numbers for illustrations are in **boldface**